THE FOUR MUSICIANS

from the Brothers Grimm

Longman

2

A donkey worked for a farmer for a long time. At last he grew old, and he couldn't carry heavy things.

Then the farmer said: "The donkey's old. I must kill him and sell his skin." The donkey heard him.

"I must run away," the donkey thought. "My body's old, but my voice is still strong. *Hee-haw! Hee-haw!* I'll go to Bremen, and I'll be a musician there."

So that night he ran away. On the road he met a very unhappy dog.

"Hello, old dog!" said the donkey. "Why are you sad?"

The dog said: "I'm old now, and I can't help my master on his farm. He wanted to kill me, so I ran away. But what can I do now?"

"Come with me," the donkey said. "I'm going to Bremen, and we can be musicians there. A dog and a donkey can sing together nicely."

"*Wroof! Wroof!* I'll come with you."

The donkey and the dog went along the road. After a time, they saw a very unhappy cat.

"Hello, old cat!" said the donkey. "Why are you sad?"

"I'm old," said the cat. "I sleep near the fire, and I don't catch mice. So the farmer's wife doesn't want me. But what can I do now?"

"Come with us. We're going to Bremen. We're going to be musicians there."

"*Miaow! Miaow!* I'll come with you."

The three animals went along the road. After a time, they saw an unhappy old cock.

"Hello, old cock!" said the donkey. "Why are you sad?"

"I'm old, but my voice is still strong. I wake the farmer and his wife every morning. Why do they want to cook me for supper? What can I do?"

"Come with us. We're going to be musicians in Bremen."
"*Cock-a-doodle-doo!* Yes, I'll come with you."

9

The four animals went along the road.
Night came, and they were tired.

11

The donkey and the dog lay down
under a tree. The cat went up
into the tree. And the cock
flew to the top of the tree.
  From the top of the tree,
the cock saw a light.

"There's a house there," the cock called.

"Let's go," the donkey said. "Perhaps there's some nice dry grass."

"And some meat," the dog said.

"And some milk," the cat said.

"And some corn," the cock said.

So they walked through the forest towards the light.

The light was in a window.

"I'm the tallest," the donkey said. "I'll look through the window."

"What can you see?" the other animals asked.

"Money," said the donkey. "Gold and silver and precious things. It's a robbers' house. They have stolen the gold and silver and precious things. And now the three robbers are at supper. They are sitting at a table, and I can see food and drink on it."

"Food!" said the dog.

"And drink!" said the cat.

"Can't we drive them away?" the cock said.

So they made a plan. The dog jumped on the donkey's back. The cat climbed on the dog's back. The cock flew up and stood on the cat's back.

Then the donkey said: "Now!" And they broke the glass of the window – *CRASH!*

They sang their loudest songs together:
"HEE-HAW! HEE-HAW! WROOF! WROOF!
MIAOW! MIAOW! COCK-A-DOODLE-DOO!"

"Help!" the robbers cried. "A terrible monster!"
And they ran out of the house and into the forest.

The animals sat down at the table, and they ate all the food. Then they put out the light and they found places to sleep.

The donkey lay down on some dry grass outside. The dog found a mat near the door. The cat liked a place near the fire. And the cock flew up onto the roof.

The robbers saw the house without a light.
"Why were we afraid?" said the head robber.
"You, Ernst, go to the house and look."
So Ernst went slowly back to the house.

The house was quiet. Ernst went into the kitchen. The cat woke up and watched him. He saw her eyes, and he thought they were gold. He put his hand out ...

"*Miaow!*" screamed the cat. And she scratched his face.

"Help!" shouted Ernst. He ran towards the door – and put his foot on the dog.

"*Wroof!*" And the dog bit his leg.

"Oh!" screamed Ernst, and he ran outside.

"*Hee-haw!*" The donkey kicked him on the head.

"Ouch!" cried Ernst.

"*Cock-a-doodle-doo!*" The cock on the roof moved his wings and gave a louder "*Cock-a-doodle-doo!*"

Ernst ran back to the other robbers.
"Quickly!" he cried. "We must run away. First
a wicked witch screamed and scratched me with
her long finger nails. Then a man drove his knife
into my leg. I ran out of the house, and a terrible
monster hit me on the head with a big club. And
the devil was on the roof. He waved his arms
and screamed: 'Cut the man in two! Cut the man
in two!'"

The robbers ran away, and they never came back.

The four old friends were very happy in the house. They stayed there and never went to Bremen.

Every evening, after supper, they sing together. It is a terrible noise, but they like it. They think they are the best musicians in the world.

Exercises

A. TRUE or FALSE

Are these sentences true about the story? Write T
(True) or F (False – not true).

For example, the answer to No. 1 is: 1F.

1   The old donkey's voice was not strong.
2   The farmer wanted to sell the donkey's skin.
3   The donkey met a very unhappy dog.
4   The cat caught mice every day.
5   The cat saw a light from the top of a tree.
6   The head robber sent Ernst to the house.

B. THE MUSICIANS' SONGS – an easy exercise

We have answered No. 1 for you.

1   The cat's song was *Miaow!*
2   The dog's song was ...
3   The cock's song was ...
4   The donkey's song was ...
5   Their four songs together were a terrible ...

C. WHAT REALLY HAPPENED TO ERNST?

Choose words from this list to go in place of the
words in brackets [ ]. For example, the answer to No.
1 is: (1) cat.

> *dog   cock   cat   donkey   teeth*
> *Cock-a-doodle-doo   claws   kicked*

First a [(1) wicked witch] scratched him with her
[(2) long finger nails]. Then a [(3) man] put his [(4)
knife] into Ernst's leg. After that, a [(5) terrible
monster] [(6) hit] Ernst on the head. And the [(7)
devil] cried [(8) "Cut the man in two!"].

D. WHO SAID IT?

Example: "Hello, old dog!" Answer: The donkey said it.

1 "I must kill him and sell his skin."
2 "The farmer's wife doesn't want me."
3 "I wake the farmer and his wife every morning."
4 "I'll look through the window."
5 "Quickly! We must run away."

E. WHY?

Example: Why did the donkey run away?
Answer: He ran away because the farmer wanted to kill him.

1 Why did the dog run away?
2 Why was the cat sad?
3 Why was the cock unhappy?
4 Why did the robbers run out of the house?
5 Why did the dog bite Ernst?

F. LET'S LOOK AT THE PICTURES AGAIN

Answer these questions about the pictures.

Pages

6	1	Is it a young cat or an old cat?
8–9	2	Does this really happen in the story?
	3	What town is it?
	4	What are the people doing?
12	5	Where is the old cock going?
13	6	The old friends are walking towards a light. What is the light?
17	7	Why are the robbers afraid?
21	8	What's the donkey doing?
	9	Who is the man in the picture?
29	10	What's the cat holding?

Longman Group Limited,
Longman House, Burnt Mill, Harlow,
Essex CM20 2JE, England
and Associated Companies throughout the world.

© Longman Group Limited 1986

First published 1986
ISBN 0 582 54118 2

Set in 14/16 pt Monophoto Univers Medium
Produced by Longman Group (FE) Ltd.
Printed in Hong Kong

English Language Teaching version by
D.K. Swan.

Illustrators: Sally Launder
           Chris McEwan
           Alastair McIlwain
           Ian Moo-Young
           Carolyn Scrace
           Alison de Vere